TABLE OF CONTENTS

Player

Wade Boggs .... Red Sox

Jose Canseco .... A's

Kirk Gibson .... Dodgers

Mark Grace .... Cubs

Mike Greenwell .... Red Sox

Orel Hershiser .... Dodgers

Don Mattingly .... Yankees

Mark McGwire .... A's

Kirby Puckett .... Twins

Chris Sabo .... Reds

Ozzie Smith .... Cardinals

Darryl Strawberry .... Mets

WADE BOGGS

Born: June 15, 1958, at Omaha, Nebraska
Height: 6′2″
Weight: 197
College: Hillsborough Community College
High School: Tampa, Florida; H.B. Plant

The unperturbed one might be the best way to describe Boston Red Sox third baseman Wade Boggs. His life has been a series of mishaps off the field, yet nothing seems to affect his performance.

After the 1985 season, there was a serious illness suffered by his sister. Then, during the '86 season, his mother was killed in a car accident. Perhaps the worst came during the 1988 season when his personal life became headlines because he ended a relationship with another woman.

And yet, through it all, Boggs just kept pounding out base hits. It is as if Boggs retreats into a cocoon to prepare himself for every game. His routine never waivers. He got that way because his father was a military man, used to a precise routine.

Boggs arrives at the ballpark exactly 3½ hours before the scheduled start of the game. He puts on his uniform a certain way, his batting practice is done the same way every day and he does wind sprints on the field precisely 18 minutes before the first pitch.

And it doesn't seem to matter what teams do to defense him. Boggs, more often than not, finds a hole somewhere.

"Every team plays me differently," he said. "Some teams play me to pull, some teams play me to go the other way, some play me to go up the middle. They're all different."

But not very successful. Since 1983, he has led the American League in hitting in five of the six seasons through 1988. In '88, he not only led the league with a .366 average, but also had the most doubles in the league with 45 and scored the most runs (128).

If there's one major leaguer capable of hitting .400, it is Boggs. But he doesn't think about it.

"I don't think much about hitting .400 because I don't think down the road or anything like that. The last day of the season, if I'm close to hitting .400, then it'll probably enter my mind," he said.

With all the distractions, it's easy to see that nothing extraneous enters his mind. So focused, Boggs just concentrates on one thing: hitting a baseball. And that is something he does better than anyone.

Batting Statistics

	AB	H	2B	3B	HR	RBI	Avg.
Career-7 Years	3913	1392	263	29	61	469	.356

33

JOSE CANSECO

Born: July 2, 1964, at Havana, Cuba
Height: 6′3″
Weight: 230

The night of September 23, 1988, will be one Oakland A's outfielder Jose Canseco will forever remember. On that night against the Milwaukee Brewers, Canseco stole two bases to give him 40 for the season, making him the first player in the history of major league baseball to hit 40 or more home runs and steal 40 or more bases in the same season.

"This is probably the biggest night of my career," he said later. "I got the base and I got the ball. That's quite an achievement for one night."

Oddly, when Canseco said he was pursuing the 40-40 goal during spring training, he didn't realize no one had ever done it.

"I figured five or six players must have done it," he said. The closest was Bobby Bonds of the San Francisco Giants in 1973. He stole 43 bases, but went the last 21 games of the season without a homer and finished with 39.

Said A's Manager Tony LaRussa, "It's got to be on the list of top five or 10 achievements in history."

A's coach Bob Watson put Canseco's season in perspective. "I've seen some players put together some big numbers, but when the game was out of hand," Watson said. "Jose has hit some big home runs and he has stolen bases when we needed them. And what's amazing is that he's only 24 years old."

Canseco finished the '88 season with 42 home runs, an American League high, and 40 stolen bases. He also drove in a league-high 124 runs and batted .307 as the A's reached the World Series before being upset by the Los Angeles Dodgers.

Most remarkable is that Canseco has put such big numbers together playing in a home stadium not conducive to power hitters. Of his 111 career home runs, almost 60 percent have come on the road.

Another milestone he reached during 1988 was becoming the first player since Chuck Klein of the Philadelphia Phillies in 1929-31 to hit at least 30 homers in each of his first three seasons.

Canseco hit 33 in 1986, 31 in '87 and the 42 in '88. His RBI totals have also been consistent: 117, 113 and 124.

However, what he was most proud of was getting his average over .300 after hitting .240 and .257 in his first two full seasons. It was no surprise when he was named the American League's Most Valuable Player in 1988 by the Baseball Writers of America.

Batting Statistics

	AB	H	2B	3B	HR	RBI	Avg.
Career-4 Years	1936	522	102	4	111	367	.270

LA
Dodgers

KIRK GIBSON

Born: May 28, 1957, at Pontiac, Michigan
Height: 6′3″
Weight: 215
College: Michigan State University

It will be one of those magic memories in World Series history that will be treasured for generations. Tormented by a knee injury, Los Angeles Dodgers outfielder Kirk Gibson hobbled to the plate in the first game of the 1988 World Series against the Oakland A's.

The Dodgers trailed, 4-3. They were up in the bottom of the ninth, with one man on and two out, and Manager Tommy LaSorda called Gibson's number.

And with one swing, Kirk Gibson became a part of Series lore forever. He blasted a game-winning home run that no Hollywood writer could have scripted any better. It was his only at-bat of the Series, and the Dodgers went on to win in five games.

Of course, Gibson did his most damage during the regular season when he hit .290 with 25 homers and 76 RBI. But it wasn't only the numbers that made him stand out. In fact, the figures are solid, but unspectacular.

But Gibson brought a new attitude to the Dodgers and it paid off with a divisional title. Before he was acquired as a free agent prior to the '88 season, the Dodgers had been below .500 in 1986 and '87. It was mostly those intangibles that produced a National League MVP award in a close vote between him and Darryl Strawberry of the New York Mets.

Standout pitcher Orel Hershiser said Gibson "made it cool to work hard and be a hustler."

Gibson's statistics become more significant when it's realized that he was playing his first year in the National League after nine in the American. Some predicted a rocky road adjusting to the new league. "People will say I don't know the pitchers," he said before the '88 season, "but they don't know me either. If I was afraid of it, I wouldn't have changed.

"I have ability. I can't worry about the negatives. I'm sure I'll prove human, but in the long run I think I'll be a positive influence on this club."

He was right on one account and wrong on the other. He was a positive influence on the Dodgers. But that "human" stuff was forgotten on an unforgettable World Series night in California.

Batting Statistics

	AB	H	2B	3B	HR	RBI	Avg.
Career—10 Years	3752	1042	168	36	175	575	.278

MARK GRACE

Born: June 28, 1964, at Winston-Salem, North Carolina
Height: 6′2″
Weight: 190
Colleges: Saddleback College and San Diego State University

Scouting is certainly an imperfect science. Clearly, though it's not really a science. That helps explain how a 24th-round draft choice in 1985 can become The Sporting News National League Rookie Player of the Year three years later.

Grace was first drafted by the Minnesota Twins' organization in January 1984, in the 15th round of the amateur draft. And the January draft is usually not as deep in talent as the June draft.

Grace remained in college and 18 months later, in June 1985, the Cubs snatched him on the 24th round. That means almost 600 players were drafted before him.The Cubs knew they had something special as soon as he started making quick stops in the minors. He was too good to stay in one place too long.

In 1986, his first year in the minors, Grace led the Midwest League in hitting with a .342 average. Playing for Peoria, Grace also hit 15 homers with 95 RBI. The next year, for Pittsfield in the Eastern League, Grace batted. 333, led the league in RBI with 101 and hit 17 homers.

While his rookie-of-the year season produced only seven homers, all on the road, he did hit .296 and drove in 57 runs. But Grace believes as he improves and matures, the homers will come.

"I was kind of feeling my way around last year," he said. "Guys I'd been reading about and watching on TV were suddenly my teammates. Then, two months after I got here, I batted third. That kind of blew me away. I was hitting behind Ryne Sandberg and ahead of Andre Dawson. I was the middle of an MVP sandwich."

Cubs General Manager Jim Frey believes Grace will be the MVP one day.

"Don Mattingly didn't hit for power in the minors," Frey said. "When he came up to the Yankees, they said, 'Who needs a singles hitter to left field?' Suddenly, he was a power hitter. Stan Musial, same thing. No one thought he'd hit (homers) like that.

"It came later for them. Maybe it will come later for Mark Grace. We think it will, and so does he."

Batting Statistics

	AB	H	2B	3B	HR	RBI	Avg.
Career—1 Year	486	144	23	4	7	57	.296

B
RED SO

MIKE GREENWELL

Born: July 18, 1963, at Louisville, Kentucky
Height: 6′0″
Weight: 195

Mike Greenwell has always been a battler, always having to prove himself. But the fight paid off, although it took an injury to give him the chance he believed he always deserved.

In late June of 1987, Greenwell got the opportunity to play every day in left field when Jim Rice was injured. Greenwell has been impossible to keep out of the lineup since.

In just 125 games and 412 at-bats in '87, Greenwell had 31 doubles, 19 homers and 89 runs batted in to go along with a batting average of .328. His next season was more of the same, although the 1988 figures represented a complete season.

Greenwell played in 158 games, smacking 39 doubles, 22 homers, knocking in 119 runs and batting .325.

To understate the obvious, Mike Greenwell can hit a baseball. That was evident from the day he first stepped foot into the major leagues. The time was September 1985. And Greenwell had been called up from the minors for the last month of the season. He wanted to make it a memorable month.

All he did was blast a game-winning, two-run homer against Toronto in his first major league at-bat. Not finished, the next night he hit another two-run, game-winning home run. Just for good measure, Greenwell's third hit was a homer, too, although not a game-decider.

Still, he was concerned about getting that opportunity to play. In his brief 17-game appearance in '85, he batted 31 times, registered 10 hits (one double and four homers), drove in eight runs and hit .323.

But he started the '86 season in the minors, and started tinkering with things after being called up to the Red Sox during the season. He changed his batting style and still hit .314 in just 35 at-bats. But he felt his power was reduced (no homers in the 11 hits) and struck out too much.

Back to the original way the next spring, that led to his '87 explosion on the major league scene.

In the off-season, Greenwell hunts alligators. "I like to slip up behind them, grab them by the tail and flip them over," he said. "Dangerous? Not if you know what you're doing."

Kind of like hitting a baseball.

Batting Statistics

	AB	H	2B	3B	HR	RBI	Avg.
Career—4 Years	1068	348	73	14	45	220	.326

LA
Dodgers
55

OREL HERSHISER

Born: September 16, 1958, at Buffalo, New York
Height: 6′3″
Weight: 190
College: Bowling Green State University

Just like the Army slogan, Los Angeles Dodgers Pitcher Orel Hershiser has a simple outlook regarding his performance as an athlete.

"I'll be the best that I can be," Hershiser has said. "That's the standard I set for myself. That's the standard I always set for myself. What the rest of the baseball world sets for me may be something else. But in 1986, when everyone said I had an off year (14-14), I didn't agree, because I still did the best that I could."

In 1988, Hershiser's best was better than most who have ever tried to master the pitcher's mound. He helped pitch the Dodgers to the world's championship, acknowledging that "winning was a total team effort, not just one guy," but also realizing his own numbers were simply staggering.

Hershiser led the National League with 267 innings pitched and tied for the most victories with 23, while losing just eight. His earned run average was a sparkling 2.26. Most memorable, however, was a season-ending streak of 59 consecutive scoreless innings, breaking former Dodger Don Drysdale's mark of 58. The streak was unofficially extended another eight innings before he allowed two runs against the New York Mets in the first game of the championship series.

ERAs of 1.09 in the playoffs and 1.00 in the World Series followed. Hershiser pitched a four-hitter in the 5-2 clinching World Series win. And although he won just one of three starts in the championship series, Hershiser recorded an important save when he got the final out in the fourth game, 5-4 win over the Mets. He was the seventh pitcher of the game for the Dodgers, and the last out came with the bases loaded in the bottom of the 12th inning.

"A lot of good things have happened at one time," he said, after walking away with virtually every post-season award: Cy Young Award and the Most Valuable Player in both the championship series and World Series.

He concluded, "It hasn't been just one accomplishment. When you put it all together it does make for a special season."

Pitching Statistics

	Won	Lost	SO	BB	ERA
Career—6 Years	83	49	833	357	2.77

DON MATTINGLY

Born: April 20, 1961, at Evansville, Indiana
Height: 6′0″
Weight: 175
High School: Evansville, Indiana; Memorial

It was a year New York Yankees first baseman was happy to see end. It was a year filled with controversy, an 18-day stay on the disabled list and, worst of all, less than impressive statistics.

But that's what happens when you're perceived as one of the best pure hitters in baseball. Everyone expects your performance to be automatic.

All Mattingly did in 1988 was hit .311 with 18 home runs and 88 runs batted in. For Don Mattingly, it was the equivalent of hitting .200. From 1985-1987, he hit 30 or more home runs each season for a total of 96, including 30 in 1987. The dropoff there was 12. He had put together four consecutive seasons of driving in more than 100 runs, including a league-leading total of 145 in 1985. The RBI total fell from 115 to 88 in one season.

The controversy occurred because of the media intensity of playing in New York. Every incident becomes headlines in the tabloid newspapers.

In Mattingly's case, a war of words began with club owner George Steinbrenner, who has always been quick to put the rap on players who aren't performing.

Mattingly responded by saying the team's slump occurred because the owner didn't respect the players. Steinbrenner took it all with a grain of salt, although there were rumors Mattingly might be traded.

But when the 1989 season opened, Mattingly was still in New York, hoping to erase the bad memories of the year before. Even if many players would be quite pleased if their production matched Mattingly's 1988 numbers.

But Mattingly realizes he must be counted on to help the Yankees.

"What I do give this team is consistency," he said. "I'm one of those guys you can count on every day during the course of the season, and you need that."

Batting Statistics

	AB	H	2B	3B	HR	RBI	Avg.
Career—6 Years	3391	1109	235	13	141	604	.327

MARK McGWIRE

Born: October 1, 1963, at Pomona, California

Height: 6′5″

Weight: 225

College: University of Southern California

High School: Claremont, California; Damien

Expectations are often enough to make solid performances pale in comparison to what has gone before. That was certainly true of the Oakland A's Mark McGwire in 1988.

Most major league players would sacrifice most anything to do what McGwire did in his second full season: bat .260, slam 32 home runs and drive in 99 runs. But coming off a rookie year when he hit .289 with 49 homers and 118 RBI, the expectations were that he would easily match those numbers. Astute observers knew that was near impossible.

"I think I had a pretty darn good year," said McGwire, who was also going through a divorce during the season. "I was third in the league in home runs, in the top eight in runs batted in and second in the league in game-winning RBI (20).

"I think people looked at me more for what I didn't do compared to 1987. I don't think that's fair."

Said Manager Tony LaRussa, "When you look at consistent run production, he had a great year."

LaRussa also noted how McGwire dealt with the pressures of being on a division-winning team as well as the personal troubles he was experiencing.

"Mark McGwire has shown in his first years that he is amazing," LaRussa said. "He's one of the amazing A's; he's just a strong guy mentally."

Not bad for a player who began his college career as a pitcher. That was where Southern Cal Coach Rod Dedeaux wanted him, but in the summer of 1982, assistant coach Ron Vaughn began working with McGwire and turned him into a hitter.

Dedeaux still believes McGwire is a good enough athlete to pitch effectively in the majors.

"I think he's still a major league prospect as a pitcher," he said. "But with that bat in his hands, he's awesome."

Meanwhile, other pitchers still have to try to figure out ways to get McGwire out. And McGwire still strives to get better.

"There is always room for improvement, definitely as a hitter," McGwire said.

And that's definitely bad news for American League hurlers.

Batting Statistics

	AB	H	2B	3B	HR	RBI	Avg.
Career—3 Years	1160	314	51	5	84	226	.271

34

KIRBY PUCKETT

Born: March 14, 1961, at Chicago, Illinois
Height: 5′8″
Weight: 210
Colleges: Bradley University and Triton Junior College
High School: Chicago, Illinois; Calumet

Athletes are asked many questions during the course of the long, 162-game season. But Minnesota Twins center fielder Kirby Puckett remembers what he was once asked by someone who pushed a microphone in his face.

The interviewer wondered, "Kirby, what is your philosophy of playing center field?"

Puckett thought for a moment, then said simply, "Catch everything."

It's not much different from his overall philosophy of playing the game he loves.

"At the plate, swing at everything," he has said. "Play hard every day. That's it."

He's been doing just that since becoming a regular in 1984. That season was only a glimpse of what was to come. In 128 games, Puckett hit .296, but hit no homers and drove in just 31 runs in 557 at bats. It looked like he might be a good hitter for average, but with little power. The following season, he led the league with 691 at bats, hit a solid .288 but had just four home runs and 74 RBI.

The new Puckett emerged after lengthy hours working with batting coach Tony Oliva during spring training in 1986. Oliva suggested that Puckett move closer to the plate, keep his weight back and then move into the pitch with a high leg kick.

"When you want to be good at something, it takes a while," Puckett said. "But it worked out pretty good."

Now, there's an understatement. From 1986-88, Puckett hit a total of 83 homers, drove in 316 runs and put together batting averages of .328, .332 and .356.

He was simply unstoppable in '88 with that .356 average, 24 homers and 121 RBI. He not only led the American League with 234 hits and 657 at bats but also led all outfielders in put outs with 450.

But Puckett has remained unpretentious. "I'm the same person as I always was," he says. "The big money hasn't changed me. I have more material things, but I'm the same person I was when I was 12 years old."

Except now, he terrorizes pitchers.

Batting Statistics

	AB	H	2B	3B	HR	RBI	Avg.
Career—5 Years	3209	1028	152	34	87	421	.320

Louisville Slugger
Franklin

CHRIS SABO

Born: January 19, 1962, at Detroit, Michigan
Height: 6′0″
Weight: 185
College: University of Michigan

The Rookie of the Year in the National League, according to the Baseball Writers of America, was a guy who grew up wanting to play in the National Hockey League.

Growing up in Detroit, Chris Sabo, was a goalkeeper on two national championship teams. He played baseball also but wasn't selected until the 30th round of the June 1980 amateur draft by the Montreal Expos.

So Sabo decided to play baseball for the University of Michigan and become an All-American player. That led to being a 2nd-round choice of the Cincinnati Reds in the June 1983 draft.

He played five seasons in the minors before earning a spot on the Red's roster in 1988 thanks to knee surgery undergone in the off-season by regular third baseman Buddy Bell.

"I'm just here to make the club, win a utility spot," Sabo had said before the start of spring training. But Bell wasn't ready for the opening of the season and Sabo got the start. He suddenly made Bell expendable, and Bell was traded in June.

"He loves to play—and it shows," says Reds Manager Pete Rose. "He approaches the game the way you are supposed to, the way it seems like everybody did 15 years ago. There is nothing phony about him. He hustles whether he is 4 for 4 or 0 for 4. You almost love to watch him make an out, because he hates it so much."

A big thrill in his rookie season was being named to the All-Star Team for the game to be played in Cincinnati. He took in stride the fact he was only used as a pinch-runner in the game, and never got to play in the field.

"Hey, I did my thing," he said. "I got to play and I stole a base, put myself in scoring position. I'm a rookie, you know."

Sabo readily admits his work ethic comes courtesy of his father. Said Sabo, "My father worked hard all his life, still does. He taught me to work hard and always told me, 'As long as you work hard and are a producer, somebody out there will always want you.'"

Right now, the Reds are the lucky ones.

Batting Statistics

	AB	H	2B	3B	HR	RBI	Avg.
Career—1 Year	538	146	40	2	11	44	.271

OZZIE SMITH

Born: December 26, 1954, at Mobile, Alabama

Height: 5′10″

Weight: 155

College: California Polytechnic State University at San Luis Obispo

The whispers began when the 1988 season ended. Ozzie Smith is too old, some said. He's entering the last year of his contract, now is the time to trade him, others noted.

But Smith, as he did his entire career, put the talk out of his head and just concentrated on getting back on track. By his own admission, 1988 wasn't a banner year. The team slumped, and Smith's string of improving his batting average was snapped at five seasons.

But he still finished with a respectable .270 average, along with 51 RBI and a career-high 57 stolen bases. Not bad for a guy who baseball experts said would never be a solid hitter.

All along the way, Smith has had something to prove to the experts. He began his career with the San Diego Padres, but was traded to the St. Louis Cardinals after the 1981 season. All the Cardinals did was win the World Series in his first season. In Smith's seven St. Louis seasons, the Cardinals have won three National League titles and that one world championship.

The winner of nine consecutive Gold Gloves for his play at shortstop, Smith didn't want to be known as a one-dimensional player. Through 1984, his highest batting average for a season was .257. The next year, it went to .276, then .280. Prior to the 1987 season, he kept working, and added weight and strength in a special program. The results were obvious.

In 1987, Smith topped the .300 mark (.303) and drove in 75 runs. Even though the average dipped in '88, he still managed to hit three home runs.

Individual statistics aside, Smith is most proud of the team's winning record and its usual competitiveness.

"The important thing is having a chance to win," he said.

But there is always the defense. The great plays become expected when you watch Ozzie Smith every day. Perhaps Los Angeles Times columnist Jim Murray penned the most fitting words to describe him.

Murray wrote, "The turf between second and third on any diamond he plays becomes the Land of Oz. Other guys play shortstop. Ozzie plays over the rainbow. It's his yellow brick road."

Batting Statistics

	AB	H	2B	3B	HR	RBI	Avg.
Career—11 Years	5914	1506	246	43	16	500	.255

Franklin